Fire Trucks

by Valerie Bodden

CREATIVE PAPERBACKS

RESCUE VEHICLES

Published by **Creative Paperbacks**
P.O. Box 227, Mankato, Minnesota 56002
Creative Paperbacks is an imprint of The Creative Company
www.thecreativecompany.us

Design and production by **Rob & Damia Design**
Art direction by **Rita Marshall**
Printed by Corporate Graphics in the United States of America

Photographs by **Alamy** (David R. Frazier Photolibrary, Inc., JoeFoxNewYork),
Dreamstime (Aaron Johnson), **Getty Images** (Michael Blann, Andy Caulfield,
Code Red, Hulton Archive, Gilles Mingasson/Liaison, Simone Mueller,
Orlando/Three Lions, Bob Peterson, Siede Preis), **iStockphoto** (Paul Laliberte,
Sabina Salihbasic, Marek Slusarczyk), **Rob & Damia Design** (Damia Stewart)

The Library of Congress has cataloged the hardcover edition as follows:

Bodden, Valerie.
Fire trucks / by Valerie Bodden.
p. cm. — (Rescue vehicles)
Summary: A fundamental introduction to ground-borne rescue vehicles
known as fire trucks, including their history, a description of their features,
and how they help people in emergencies.
Includes index.
ISBN 978-1-60818-006-6 (hardcover)
ISBN 978-0-89812-577-1 (pbk)
1. Fire engines—Juvenile literature.
2. Emergency vehicles—Juvenile literature. I. Title. II. Series.

TH9372.B63 2011
628.9'259—dc22   2009048827
CPSIA: 012411 PO1420

9 8 7 6 5 4 3 2

Contents

Sometimes people need help. They might be hurt. Or they might be lost. When people need help putting out a fire, a fire truck might come to help them.

Fire trucks zoom down the street to reach fires quickly

A fire truck is an **emergency** vehicle. It is used to put out fires. Even though fire trucks are big, they can go very fast!

These Engins, (which are

JOHN KEELI

The first fire trucks were used about 400 years ago. They were tanks of water pulled by people or by horses. About 100 years ago, people built the first fire trucks with **motors**.

Today, most fire trucks are red, yellow, or green. They have flashing lights and loud sirens (*SY-runs*). The lights and sirens warn other drivers to move out of the way.

Many fire trucks today carry ladders on top and hoses inside

Different kinds of fire trucks carry different things. Ladder trucks have a tall ladder attached to the top. Pumper trucks have pumps for spraying water. Tanker trucks have huge tanks filled with water.

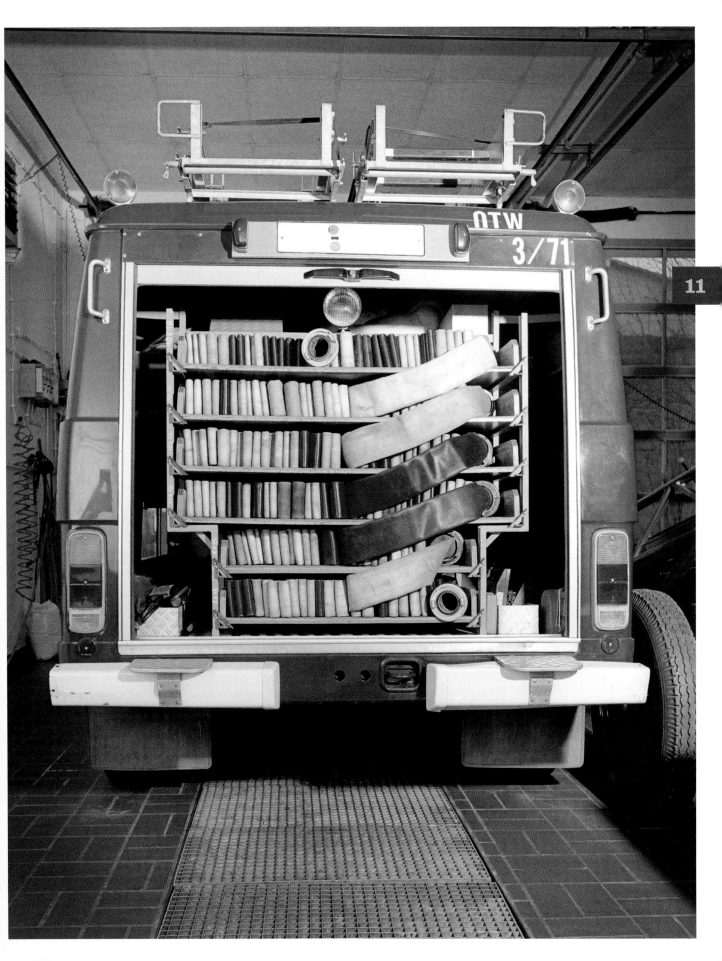

When there is a fire, an alarm goes off at the fire station. The firefighters put on their **protective** clothes and jump into the fire trucks! One firefighter drives each truck. Other firefighters sit next to or behind the driver. A **dispatcher** tells the firefighters where to go.

Firefighters practice getting their gear on very quickly

When the fire trucks get to the fire, some firefighters hook up the hoses. They can hook up the hoses to a **fire hydrant** or to a tank on the pumper or tanker truck. The firefighters begin spraying water on the fire.

Firefighters wear helmets and heavy gloves when using a hose

Some firefighters climb ladders to put out fires in tall buildings. They can rescue people trapped in buildings, too. Firefighters wear air masks to help them breathe inside burning buildings.

When firefighters cannot enter through doors, they use ladders

After the fire is out, the firefighters drive the fire trucks back to the station. They wash the trucks and check their gear. They make sure the fire trucks are ready for the next emergency!

Firefighters in the 1860s (above); a steam-powered pump truck and 1950s fire engine (right)

Early Fire Trucks

The first fire trucks were just big tanks of water. People had to pump the water by hand to get it out of the tank. Then, people made pumps that were powered by steam. These pumps worked faster. They were more powerful, too. They could spray more water out of hoses.

Glossary

dispatcher

a person whose job is to get phone calls about emergencies and then send out rescue vehicles

emergency

something bad that happens suddenly, such as a car accident or fire

fire hydrant

a water pipe that sticks out of the ground; firefighters can attach a hose to it

motors

machines that make things, such as cars, move

protective

able to keep people safe